Fairy Tale Creatures

Ogres

by Emma Huddleston

FOCUS READERS

BEACON

www.focusreaders.com

Focus Readers is distributed by North Star Editions:
sales@northstareditions.com | 888-417-0195

Produced for Focus Readers by Red Line Editorial.

Photographs ©: Shutterstock Images, cover, 1, 4, 8, 10, 16, 18, 20, 23, 24, 26–27, 29; iStockphoto, 6, 13; John Martin/Alamy, 14

Library of Congress Cataloging-in-Publication Data
Names: Huddleston, Emma, author.
Title: Ogres : fairy tale creatures / by Emma Huddleston.
Description: Lake Elmo, MN : Focus Readers, [2022] | Series: Fairy tale creatures | Includes index. | Audience: Grades 2-3
Identifiers: LCCN 2021010621 (print) | LCCN 2021010622 (ebook) | ISBN 9781637390061 (hardcover) | ISBN 9781637390139 (paperback) | ISBN 9781637390207 (ebook) | ISBN 9781637390269 (pdf)
Subjects: LCSH: Ghouls and ogres--Juvenile literature.
Classification: LCC GR560 .H84 2022 (print) | LCC GR560 (ebook) | DDC 398.21--dc23
LC record available at https://lccn.loc.gov/2021010621
LC ebook record available at https://lccn.loc.gov/2021010622

Printed in the United States of America
Mankato, MN
082021

About the Author

Emma Huddleston lives in Minnesota with her husband. She enjoys writing children's books and spending time outside. She also likes reading fairy tales and mysteries.

Table of Contents

Chapter 1

Danger in the Woods

Seven brothers were lost in the woods. They knew an ogre lived nearby. So, they needed somewhere safe to spend the night. The brothers walked and walked. Finally, they saw a cabin.

Many fairy tales are about children who get lost in the woods.

Ogres often carry large clubs or other weapons.

The boys knocked on the door. A woman let them inside. But she warned them. Her husband was an ogre. And he would be back soon.

Suddenly, the boys heard heavy footsteps outside the door. It was the ogre!

The boys hid under the bed, but the ogre found them. He grabbed the boys and tried to eat them. But his wife convinced him to wait until morning. While he slept, the boys crept outside and ran away.

Fun Fact

Sometimes humans turn into ogres because of curses.

PENSIERO

Chapter 2

History of Ogres

The history of ogres goes back many years. In **ancient** Italy, people had a god called Orcus. Many people feared him. His body was large and hairy. Legends said he killed and ate people.

A sculpture at the Park of the Monsters in Italy shows Orcus's huge mouth.

Statues of oni or similar creatures called nio often decorate temples.

Over time, people told stories of monsters with similar traits. These creatures were often called ogres. Like Orcus, they were big, mean, and ugly.

Many **cultures** have stories of ogres. Oni appear in **folktales** from Japan. These ogres are known for being scary and evil. Their bodies are often big and strong.

In Papua New Guinea, stories tell of origorúsos. These ogres walk on four legs. They live underground or in trees. But they **raid** villages.

Fun Fact

An origorúso has huge ears. It can use them as a blanket.

Their huge mouths can swallow people whole.

Other tales come from Europe. In the late 1600s, a French man wrote a book of children's stories. The book was called *Tales of Mother Goose*. It was based on old folktales. It used the word *ogre* for monsters that ate people.

The stories became very popular in Europe. Tales about ogres continued to spread. By the 1700s, legends of ogres were common in

People read stories of ogres out loud to their children.

Great Britain. These creatures were said to eat children. The stories warned children not to go far from home.

Chapter 3

Big and Ugly

Ogres are strong and tall. They are similar to giants. But ogres tend to be uglier. They often have green or blue skin. Their bodies may be covered in hair. Many ogres have hooked noses, too.

Most ogres have big heads and hairy bodies.

People often wear oni masks when celebrating the Japanese festival Setsubun.

In Japan, oni have horns. Their skin is often pink, red, or blue. Oni have three toes on each foot. Some oni have three eyes as well.

In England, legends said many scary ogres roamed the land. Some had two or three heads. One was a giant who carried a large bag. He grabbed children and stuffed them inside. Then he ate them.

Ogres have big appetites. They can eat huge amounts of food. And they love to eat raw meat.

Fun Fact

A cyclops is a type of ogre. It has one eye in the middle of its face.

A female ogre is called an ogress.

Ogres have large mouths and long, sharp teeth. In addition, ogres have a strong sense of smell. They can tell if people or animals are nearby.

Some ogres have special powers. For example, some ogres can shape-shift. They can change into different kinds of animals.

In one story, an ogre turns into a lion to attack. But then the ogre gets tricked into turning into a mouse. A cat eats it.

Fun Fact

One story tells of an ogre with feathers. The feathers are magical. They can **cure** sickness.

Chapter 4

Eating People

In most stories, ogres are mean monsters. They attack homes and villages. Ogres steal and eat **livestock**. But their main source of food is people. In many stories, ogres chase and catch children.

A fountain in Switzerland shows an ogre eating children.

Others try to trap people or keep them as prisoners.

Ogres often live in lonely places. Some make their homes in the woods. Others live in mountains and caves. Most ogres are not very smart. People can trick them and escape. For example, people can use **disguises**. The ogres get

Fun Fact

Many ogres live alone. But some have families.

Ogres live in swamps or other dark places.

confused. They attack or eat the wrong things.

Other ogres are more intelligent. These ogres can be rich and powerful. They may live in huge houses or castles. But they still tend to be tricky and mean.

One popular story tells of a cat that outsmarts an ogre.

Some ogres are greedy. They hoard treasure. Other ogres capture people. However, people can outsmart them and get away. In several stories, people challenge an ogre to a contest. If the ogre loses, the people can go free.

In rare cases, ogres can be friendly. They live with people or marry humans. A few stories are even funny. Stories about ogres continue to change. People keep creating new versions.

Fun Fact

One ogre had magic boots. Anyone who wore them could go 21 miles (34 km) in one step.

STORY SPOTLIGHT

Shrek

The Shrek **series** includes **characters** from many fairy tales. The main character is Shrek. He is an ogre. He is big and strong. And he has bright-green skin.

Shrek lives alone in a swamp. He scares away people who annoy him. He takes mud showers and eats bugs. But unlike other ogres, he doesn't eat people. Under his ugly looks, he has a kind heart.

Shrek helps a princess named Fiona. Because of a curse, she turns into an ogre every night. Shrek and Fiona fall in love. She stays an ogre and marries him.

Shrek is the main character in several movies.

FOCUS ON

Ogres

Write your answers on a separate piece of paper.

1. Write a sentence describing the main ideas of Chapter 4.
2. If you wanted to beat an ogre in a contest, what would you challenge it to do? Why?
3. What country do legends of oni come from?
   - **A.** France
   - **B.** Japan
   - **C.** Papua New Guinea
4. Why would people trick ogres instead of trying to fight them?
   - **A.** Ogres are big, so tricking ogres is easier than fighting them.
   - **B.** Ogres are sleepy, so they can't stay awake.
   - **C.** Ogres are nice, so they never fight people.

5. What does **appetites** mean in this book?

*Ogres have big **appetites**. They can eat huge amounts of food.*

- **A.** desires to eat
- **B.** desires to sleep
- **C.** plans to build

6. What does **hoard** mean in this book?

*Some ogres are greedy. They **hoard** treasure.*

- **A.** to give something away
- **B.** to keep large amounts of something
- **C.** to dislike something

Answer key on page 32.

Glossary

ancient
Very old or from long ago.

characters
People in stories or movies.

cultures
Groups of people and the ways they live, including their customs, beliefs, and laws.

cure
To heal an illness or injury.

disguises
Ways of changing how you look so others won't find you or know who you are.

folktales
Stories that have been told out loud for many years.

livestock
Animals that farmers raise for the purpose of making money.

raid
To attack and steal from.

series
A set of books, movies, or stories about the same characters.

To Learn More

BOOKS

Krensky, Stephen. *The Book of Mythical Beasts & Magical Creatures*. New York: DK Publishing, 2020.

London, Martha. *Giants*. Minneapolis: Abdo Publishing, 2020.

Rowley, Kris Erickson. *Trolls*. Lake Elmo, MN: Focus Readers, 2019.

NOTE TO EDUCATORS

Visit **www.focusreaders.com** to find lesson plans, activities, links, and other resources related to this title.

Index

Answer Key: 1. Answers will vary; **2.** Answers will vary; **3.** B; **4.** A; **5.** A; **6.** B